Smelly Feet
Sandwich
and Other Silly Poems

by Allia Zobel Nolan

Illustrated by Kate Leake

tiger tales

Smelly Feet Sandwich

I am hungry. I am starving.
But I don't know what to eat.
So I sit beside the open fridge,
and stare down at my feet.

They are dirty. They are smelly.
They remind me of some cheese.
Do you think they might be tasty
on some jellied toast with peas?

It's Not Fair

Why is it
when babies go "BURP,"
everyone shouts,
"HOORAY"?
Yet I let one rip
and people get mad.
They ask, "Young man,
what do you say?"

The Wiggly Tooth

My best friend's tooth is wiggly,
and he's asked me what to do.
Should I pry it out with pliers?
Should I make him taffy stew?

I suggested he bite jawbreakers
or chew on an old shoe.
I could try making loose-tooth juice
with crunchy rocks and glue.

SNIFF

GLUE

Still, if all else fails, there's one sure thing
I know will do the trick—
I'll give him some of my mom's cake.
His tooth will come out quick.

Ah-choooooooooo!

My sneezes cause breezes
in Mexico.
I'm sure folks can feel
them in Spain.
Perhaps they cause
tremors on Jupiter.
At home, they
most likely cause rain.

I'm Not Bored Anymore!

My TV is broken.
   My book is half read.
I am boreder than bored.
   I am out of my head.

I've played dozens of video games.
   Now I'm through.
I don't really know what else
   there is to do.

"I think I can help you out, dear,"
   said my mother.
"You can rake up the leaves.
   Take that snake from your brother.

Walk the cat. Feed the fish.
   Match some socks if you please.
Change your sister, and then
   spray the ferret for fleas.

You can vacuum the hall.
   The tub needs some scrubbing.
The dog fought a skunk,
   so he'll need quite a rubbing.

Mind the baby so she doesn't
   eat her balloon.
What's the matter?" said Mom.
   "Are you leaving so soon?"

Yikes! It's Aunt Bea

When my great, old Aunt Bea
comes to visit with me,
I go quick and hide under the bed.
'Cause her voice really squeaks,
and she pinches my cheeks.
Even worse, she comes with her hog, Fred.

One day, she happened by
with some broccoli pie,
which was covered with brussels sprout jam.
I refused it on sight.
I would not take a bite.
I said, "Aunt Bea, I'd rather have ham."

My "Good to Go" Invention

Sometimes it seems I have to go,
but then I sit and wait.
Then other times I run real fast,
and hope that I'm not late.

So this is my invention. Look—
It works just like a charm.
It tells me "Now it's time to go"
or "It's a false alarm."

good to go

Quick, Does Anyone Want 25 Worms in a Shoebox?

My mother told me yesterday,
"This world is filled with germs.
And that," she said, "is why I say,
don't ever play with worms."

I dug them up the other day.
I didn't think she'd care.
But now I have to hide them all.
My problem, though, is where?

Uh-oh.... Here she comes.
GULP!
"Hi, Mom."

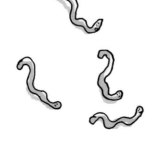
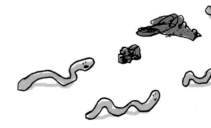

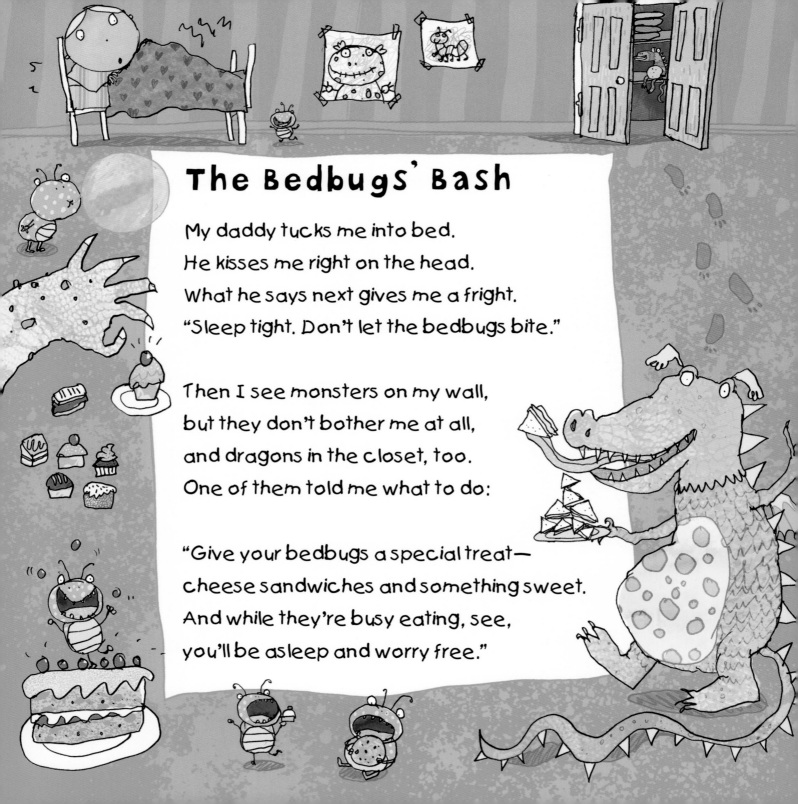

The Bedbugs' Bash

My daddy tucks me into bed.
He kisses me right on the head.
What he says next gives me a fright.
"Sleep tight. Don't let the bedbugs bite."

Then I see monsters on my wall,
but they don't bother me at all,
and dragons in the closet, too.
One of them told me what to do:

"Give your bedbugs a special treat—
cheese sandwiches and something sweet.
And while they're busy eating, see,
you'll be asleep and worry free."

So later, bugs and dragons ate,
and monsters licked clean every plate.
"Thanks, guys," a giant bedbug said.
"I much prefer this food, instead."